# THE CALM OF THE

# FOREST

## 2025 CALENDAR

# JANUARY 2025

| SUNDAY | MONDAY | TUESDAY | WEDNESDAY | THURSDAY | FRIDAY | SATURDAY |
|--------|--------|---------|-----------|----------|--------|----------|
| 29 | 30 | 31 | 1 | 2 | 3 | 4 |
| 5 | 6 | 7 | 8 | 9 | 10 | 11 |
| 12 | 13 | 14 | 15 | 16 | 17 | 18 |
| 19 | 20 | 21 | 22 | 23 | 24 | 25 |
| 26 | 27 | 28 | 29 | 30 | 31 | 1 |

# FEBRUARY 2025

| SUNDAY | MONDAY | TUESDAY | WEDNESDAY | THURSDAY | FRIDAY | SATURDAY |
|--------|--------|---------|-----------|----------|--------|----------|
| 26 | 27 | 28 | 29 | 30 | 31 | 1 |
| 2 | 3 | 4 | 5 | 6 | 7 | 8 |
| 9 | 10 | 11 | 12 | 13 | 14 | 15 |
| 16 | 17 | 18 | 19 | 20 | 21 | 22 |
| 23 | 24 | 25 | 26 | 27 | 28 | 1 |

# MARCH 2025

| SUNDAY | MONDAY | TUESDAY | WEDNESDAY | THURSDAY | FRIDAY | SATURDAY |
|---|---|---|---|---|---|---|
| 23 | 24 | 25 | 26 | 27 | 28 | 1 |
| 2 | 3 | 4 | 5 | 6 | 7 | 8 |
| 9 | 10 | 11 | 12 | 13 | 14 | 15 |
| 16 | 17 | 18 | 19 | 20 | 21 | 22 |
| 23 / 30 | 24 / 31 | 25 | 26 | 27 | 28 | 29 |

# APRIL 2025

| SUNDAY | MONDAY | TUESDAY | WEDNESDAY | THURSDAY | FRIDAY | SATURDAY |
|--------|--------|---------|-----------|----------|--------|----------|
| 30 | 31 | 1 | 2 | 3 | 4 | 5 |
| 6 | 7 | 8 | 9 | 10 | 11 | 12 |
| 13 | 14 | 15 | 16 | 17 | 18 | 19 |
| 20 | 21 | 22 | 23 | 24 | 25 | 26 |
| 27 | 28 | 29 | 30 | 1 | 2 | 3 |

# MAY 2025

| SUNDAY | MONDAY | TUESDAY | WEDNESDAY | THURSDAY | FRIDAY | SATURDAY |
|--------|--------|---------|-----------|----------|--------|----------|
| 27 | 28 | 29 | 30 | 1 | 2 | 3 |
| 4 | 5 | 6 | 7 | 8 | 9 | 10 |
| 11 | 12 | 13 | 14 | 15 | 16 | 17 |
| 18 | 19 | 20 | 21 | 22 | 23 | 24 |
| 25 | 26 | 27 | 28 | 29 | 30 | 31 |

# JUNE 2025

| SUNDAY | MONDAY | TUESDAY | WEDNESDAY | THURSDAY | FRIDAY | SATURDAY |
|--------|--------|---------|-----------|----------|--------|----------|
| 1 | 2 | 3 | 4 | 5 | 6 | 7 |
| 8 | 9 | 10 | 11 | 12 | 13 | 14 |
| 15 | 16 | 17 | 18 | 19 | 20 | 21 |
| 22 | 23 | 24 | 25 | 26 | 27 | 28 |
| 29 | 30 | 1 | 2 | 3 | 4 | 5 |

# JULY 2025

| SUNDAY | MONDAY | TUESDAY | WEDNESDAY | THURSDAY | FRIDAY | SATURDAY |
|--------|--------|---------|-----------|----------|--------|----------|
| 29 | 30 | 1 | 2 | 3 | 4 | 5 |
| 6 | 7 | 8 | 9 | 10 | 11 | 12 |
| 13 | 14 | 15 | 16 | 17 | 18 | 19 |
| 20 | 21 | 22 | 23 | 24 | 25 | 26 |
| 27 | 28 | 29 | 30 | 31 | 1 | 2 |

# AUGUST 2025

| SUNDAY | MONDAY | TUESDAY | WEDNESDAY | THURSDAY | FRIDAY | SATURDAY |
|--------|--------|---------|-----------|----------|--------|----------|
| 27 | 28 | 29 | 30 | 31 | 1 | 2 |
| 3 | 4 | 5 | 6 | 7 | 8 | 9 |
| 10 | 11 | 12 | 13 | 14 | 15 | 16 |
| 17 | 18 | 19 | 20 | 21 | 22 | 23 |
| 24 / 31 | 25 | 26 | 27 | 28 | 29 | 30 |

# SEPTEMBER 2025

| SUNDAY | MONDAY | TUESDAY | WEDNESDAY | THURSDAY | FRIDAY | SATURDAY |
|--------|--------|---------|-----------|----------|--------|----------|
| 31 | 1 | 2 | 3 | 4 | 5 | 6 |
| 7 | 8 | 9 | 10 | 11 | 12 | 13 |
| 14 | 15 | 16 | 17 | 18 | 19 | 20 |
| 21 | 22 | 23 | 24 | 25 | 26 | 27 |
| 28 | 29 | 30 | 1 | 2 | 3 | 4 |

# OCTOBER 2025

| SUNDAY | MONDAY | TUESDAY | WEDNESDAY | THURSDAY | FRIDAY | SATURDAY |
|--------|--------|---------|-----------|----------|--------|----------|
| 28 | 29 | 30 | 1 | 2 | 3 | 4 |
| 5 | 6 | 7 | 8 | 9 | 10 | 11 |
| 12 | 13 | 14 | 15 | 16 | 17 | 18 |
| 19 | 20 | 21 | 22 | 23 | 24 | 25 |
| 26 | 27 | 28 | 29 | 30 | 31 | 1 |

# NOVEMBER 2025

| SUNDAY | MONDAY | TUESDAY | WEDNESDAY | THURSDAY | FRIDAY | SATURDAY |
|--------|--------|---------|-----------|----------|--------|----------|
| 26 | 27 | 28 | 29 | 30 | 31 | 1 |
| 2 | 3 | 4 | 5 | 6 | 7 | 8 |
| 9 | 10 | 11 | 12 | 13 | 14 | 15 |
| 16 | 17 | 18 | 19 | 20 | 21 | 22 |
| 23 / 30 | 24 | 25 | 26 | 27 | 28 | 29 |

# DECEMBER 2025

| SUNDAY | MONDAY | TUESDAY | WEDNESDAY | THURSDAY | FRIDAY | SATURDAY |
|--------|--------|---------|-----------|----------|--------|----------|
| 30 | 1 | 2 | 3 | 4 | 5 | 6 |
| 7 | 8 | 9 | 10 | 11 | 12 | 13 |
| 14 | 15 | 16 | 17 | 18 | 19 | 20 |
| 21 | 22 | 23 | 24 | 25 | 26 | 27 |
| 28 | 29 | 30 | 31 | 1 | 2 | 3 |

# The Top 10 Forests in the World

1. Amazon Rainforest (South America)
The largest tropical rainforest in the world, spanning multiple countries, and home to around 10% of all known species.

2. Congo Rainforest (Central Africa)
The second-largest tropical rainforest, crucial for global biodiversity and carbon storage, home to gorillas, forest elephants, and other unique species.

3. Daintree Rainforest (Australia)
One of the oldest rainforests on Earth, filled with unique plant and animal species, including many found nowhere else.

4. Tongass National Forest (USA – Alaska)
The largest national forest in the U.S. and the largest temperate rainforest in the world, rich in old-growth trees and wildlife.

5. Białowieża Forest (Poland/Belarus)
One of the last remnants of the primeval forests that once covered much of Europe, known for its ancient trees and European bison.

6. Redwood National and State Parks (USA – California)
Home to the world's tallest trees, the coastal redwoods, a stunning landscape of old-growth forest.

7. Sundarbans Mangrove Forest (Bangladesh/India)
The largest mangrove forest in the world, a critical habitat for the endangered Bengal tiger and an important buffer against floods.

8. Valdivian Temperate Rainforest (Chile/Argentina)
A unique temperate rainforest in South America, home to ancient trees like the Alerce and diverse ecosystems.

9. Monteverde Cloud Forest Reserve (Costa Rica)
Known for its unique cloud forest ecosystem, rich biodiversity, and as a hotspot for rare and endemic species.

10. Great Bear Rainforest (Canada)
A massive temperate rainforest on the west coast of British Columbia, home to the rare Kermode "spirit bear" and other wildlife.

These forests are critical for global biodiversity, climate regulation, and ecological health.

# The 10 Best Methods of Forest Conservation

1. Afforestation and Reforestation

Afforestation: Planting trees in areas where there were no previous forests.

Reforestation: Restoring forests in deforested or degraded areas. These practices help sequester carbon, restore habitats, and increase biodiversity.

2. Sustainable Logging Practices

Using methods like selective logging (harvesting only specific trees) and reduced impact logging (minimizing environmental damage during tree extraction) to reduce the impact of timber production on forest ecosystems.

3. Establishing Protected Areas

Designating forests as national parks, nature reserves, or wildlife sanctuaries to legally protect them from logging, mining, or agricultural expansion. Governments and conservation organizations often play a role in creating these protected areas.

4. Forest Management Plans

Implementing sustainable forest management (SFM) practices that balance ecological, social, and economic needs, ensuring that forests are used responsibly without degrading the environment.

5. Promoting Agroforestry

Integrating trees into agricultural landscapes to create more sustainable farming systems. Agroforestry improves soil health, water retention, and biodiversity while providing farmers with additional income from timber or fruit trees.

6. Combatting Illegal Logging

Enforcing laws and policies to stop illegal logging, which contributes to deforestation and biodiversity loss. Satellite monitoring and stricter regulations on timber trade can reduce illegal activities.

7. Restoring Degraded Forests

Actively restoring degraded ecosystems by planting native trees, controlling invasive species, and improving soil health. This can help rebuild habitats and support wildlife recovery.

8. Reducing Demand for Unsustainable Forest Products

Encouraging the use of certified sustainable products, such as FSC-certified (Forest Stewardship Council) timber, and reducing the consumption of products linked to deforestation (e.g., palm oil, beef from deforested lands).

9. Community-based Conservation

Engaging local and indigenous communities in forest conservation efforts by providing them with sustainable livelihoods that depend on maintaining healthy forests. Local knowledge and community stewardship often result in better long-term conservation outcomes.

10. Raising Awareness and Education

Promoting forest conservation through public education and advocacy. Educating communities, governments, and consumers about the value of forests and the consequences of deforestation can create a groundswell of support for conservation initiatives.